teddy bears

abc

Once there were five small bears who were usually up to something. They could Once there were five small bears who were usually up to something. This book shows them arriving in an

susanna gretz

A & C BLACK · LONDON

a

arriving

in an airplane

b

building

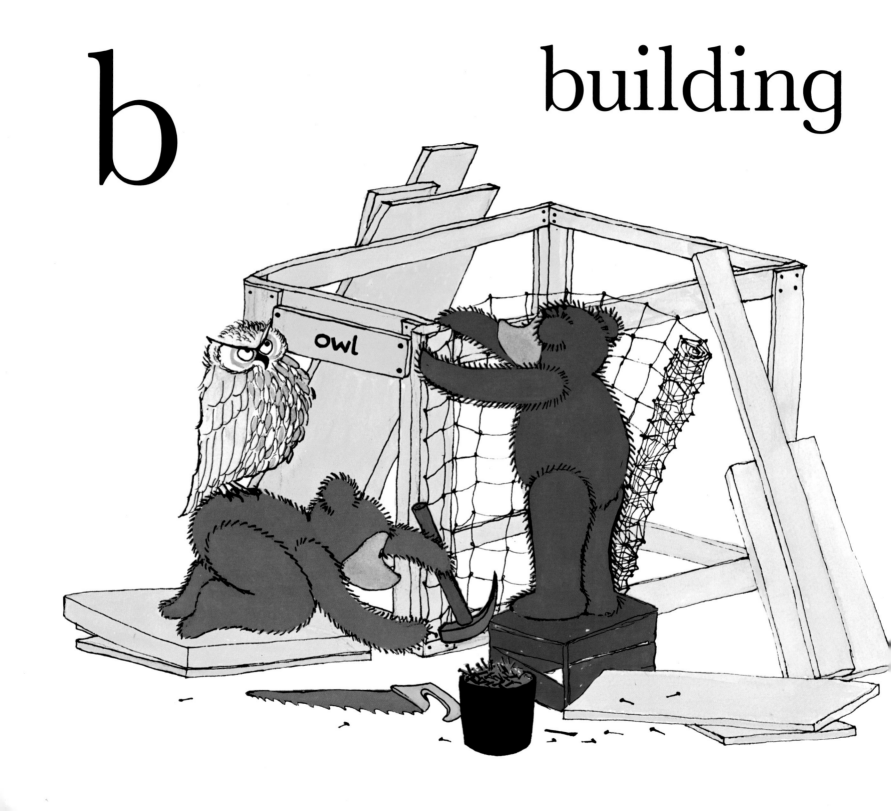

owl

C

climbing

d

dancing

e

eating

f finding fleas in their fur

g

gargling

h

hiding

i

idling

j jumping

k keeping kangaroos in the kitchen

1 leaping into the leaves

m mucking in mud

n

napping

O opening oatmeal

p

painting

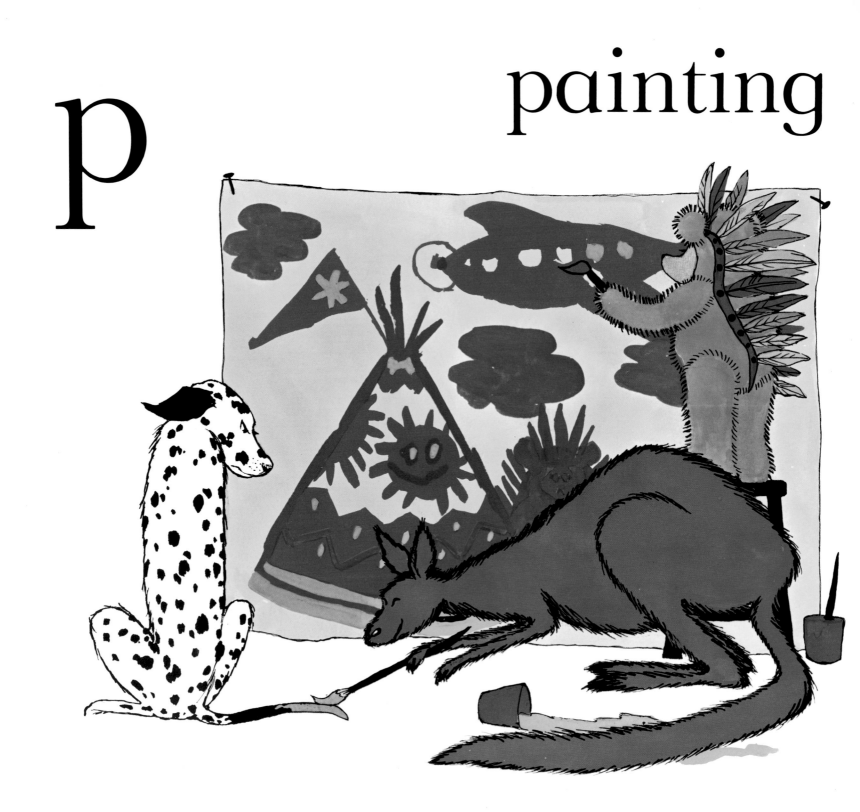

q

quarreling

r

running

in the rain

S

swimming

t

tickling in a tent

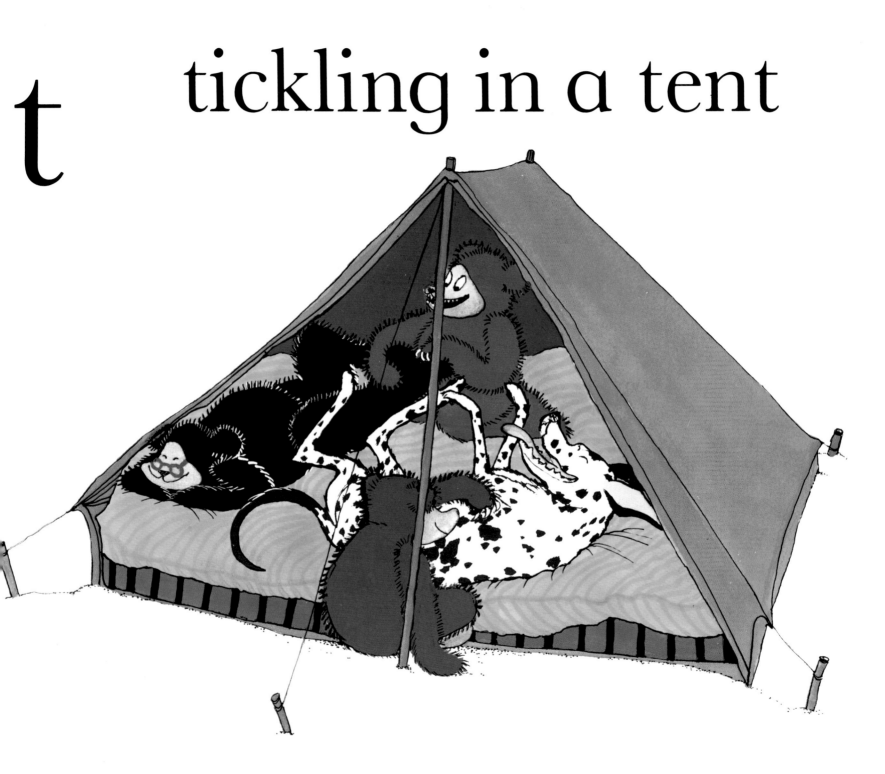

u

unwrapping an umbrella

V

vanishing

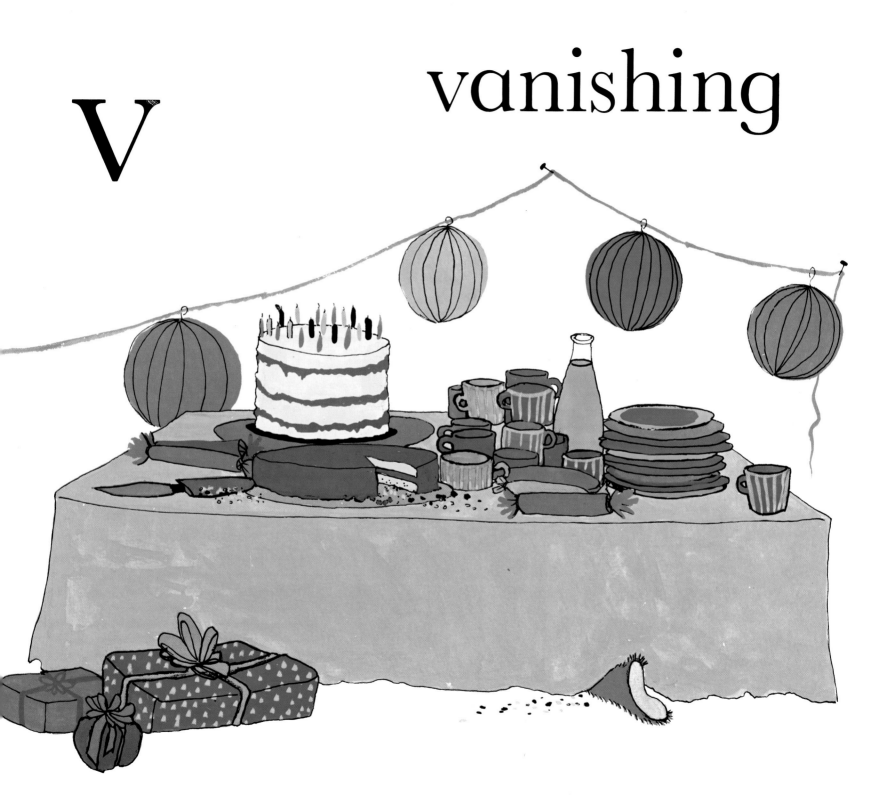

W

washing

X

being x-rayed

y   yelling at a yak

Z

zipping off

to the zoo

This edition first published in paperback in 1999
by A & C Black (Publishers) Ltd
35 Bedford Row
London WC1R 4JH

ISBN 0-7136-5225-X

First published in hardback in 1974
by Ernest Benn Limited
Reprinted 1978, 1979, 1986

Copyright © Susanna Gretz 1974